The Power of Discussion - A Guide to Using Literature Circles in the Classroom

Quick Reads for Busy Educators

Cheryl Angst

Published by Cheryl Angst, 2023.

While every precaution has been taken in the preparation of this book, the publisher assumes no responsibility for errors or omissions, or for damages resulting from the use of the information contained herein.

THE POWER OF DISCUSSION - A GUIDE TO USING LITERATURE CIRCLES IN THE CLASSROOM

First edition. May 13, 2023.

ISBN: 979-8223301226

Written by Cheryl Angst.

Also by Cheryl Angst

Quick Reads for Busy Educators
Gamifying Education - How to Engage and Motivate Students Through Games
Unlocking Gamification - Exploring the Impact and Importance in Education
Winning in the Classroom - Using Bartle's Gaming Styles to Empower Learners
Who Packed Your Parachute? Why Multiple Attempts on Assessments Matter
The Power of Discussion - A Guide to Using Literature Circles in the Classroom

Table of Contents

Introduction

AT FIRST, I WAS NERVOUS about participating in the literature circle. I didn't really like reading, and I didn't want to talk about books with other people. But my teacher assigned us to groups and gave us roles, and I found myself as the discussion leader for our group. I wasn't sure how to do it, but my teacher showed us some strategies for leading a discussion and I gave it a shot.

To my surprise, I found that I actually enjoyed talking about the book with my classmates. I learned so much from hearing their perspectives and ideas. I also found that when I had to lead the discussion, I paid more attention to the book and thought more deeply about it. I found myself making connections to other books I've read and to my own life.

One thing I really liked about the literature circle was that I had a chance to talk about things that were important to me. We talked about things like justice and friendship, and I was able to share my thoughts and opinions with others. I felt like my voice was being heard and that my ideas mattered.

Welcome to the World of Literature Circles

LITERATURE CIRCLES are a collaborative and student-centered approach to reading and discussing literature. First introduced in the 1980s, literature circles have gained popularity among educators as an effective way to engage students in critical reading, thinking, and communication skills.

At its core, literature circles involve students working in small groups to read and discuss a shared text, which can include novels, short stories, poetry, articles, and other types of literature. During literature circle meetings, students take on different roles, such as discussion director, connector, summarizer, word wizard, and literary luminary, which help guide their reading and discussions.

One of the benefits of literature circles is that they allow students to take ownership of their own learning, as they are responsible for their group's discussions and assessments. This approach promotes autonomy, as students are able to choose their own texts to read, and encourages collaboration and active participation in the classroom.

Over the years, literature circles have evolved to meet the needs of different learners, including English language learners, struggling readers, and advanced readers. The flexibility of literature circles allows teachers to differentiate instruction to meet the needs of all students, and provides opportunities for students to engage with literature in meaningful and engaging ways.

In the following chapters, we will explore the various elements of literature circles, including how to run them effectively, how to choose texts, how to assess student learning, and how to address common challenges that may arise. By the end of this book, readers will have a solid overview of how to implement literature circles in their own classrooms, and how to promote critical thinking, communication, and engagement through the power of literature.

Why Literature Circles Matter

IN RECENT YEARS, LITERATURE circles have become increasingly popular in classrooms across the country. This is because they offer a number of benefits to both teachers and students alike. In this book, we will explore why literature circles matter and what makes them an effective tool for teaching reading comprehension, critical thinking, and collaboration skills.

One of the primary benefits of literature circles is increased student engagement. When students are given the opportunity to choose their own reading material and participate in small group discussions, they are more likely to be invested in the reading process. This engagement can lead to higher levels of motivation and a deeper understanding of the material.

Literature circles can also improve reading comprehension. When students work in small groups, they are able to discuss the text in a more focused and meaningful way than they would be able to in a larger class discussion. They are able to share their thoughts and ideas with their peers, which can lead to a better understanding of the material.

In addition to improved reading comprehension, literature circles can also help develop critical thinking skills. When students are asked to analyze a text and share their interpretations with their group, they are forced to think deeply about the material and defend their ideas. This type of critical thinking is essential for success in both academic and professional settings.

Finally, literature circles can enhance collaboration skills. When students work together in small groups, they learn how to communicate effectively, listen to others' ideas, and work towards a common goal. These skills are essential for success in both the classroom and in the workforce.

Overall, literature circles offer a number of benefits to both teachers and students. They increase student engagement, improve reading comprehension, develop critical thinking skills, and enhance collaboration skills. As such, they should be a part of every teacher's toolkit for teaching reading comprehension and critical thinking.

What Are Literature Circles?

AS AN AVID READER, I was excited to join the literature circle in my class. I was looking forward to discussing books with my peers and sharing my thoughts with them. However, as we started reading and discussing, I realized that I was not being challenged enough.

At first, I was disappointed. I wanted to have deep conversations and explore complex themes, but I felt like we were just skimming the surface. However, my teacher suggested that I take on the role of the discussion leader for our next meeting. I was a bit hesitant at first, but I decided to give it a try.

As the discussion leader, I had to prepare questions that would guide the conversation and help us dive deeper into the text. I also had to make sure that everyone had a chance to speak and contribute to the discussion. It was challenging, but it was also incredibly rewarding.

Through this experience, I learned that being a good reader doesn't just mean understanding the words on the page. It means being able to think critically about what you're reading, asking questions, and making connections. It also means being able to communicate your ideas clearly and respectfully.

Participating in the literature circle not only challenged me to think more deeply about the books we were reading, but it also helped me develop my communication and leadership skills.

Literature circles are a collaborative and student-centered approach to reading instruction that can help students develop critical thinking, reading, and communication skills. In literature circles, small groups of students read the same book and meet regularly to discuss the text, share their ideas, and ask questions.

The primary goal of literature circles is to promote student engagement, ownership, and responsibility for their learning. By participating in literature circles, students have the opportunity to interact with their peers, share their thoughts, and express their opinions about the text. They can also develop their comprehension skills, such as making predictions, visualizing, questioning, inferring, and summarizing.

Literature circles have their roots in the work of educators such as Karen Smith, Frank Smith, and Donal Doherty, who first developed the concept in the 1980s. Since then, literature circles have gained popularity and have been used in classrooms across the country. The approach has been adapted and modified over time to meet the needs of diverse student populations, including English language learners, struggling readers, and advanced readers.

There are many variations for running literature circles, but at its core the teacher assigns a text to a group of students, and each student has a specific role or job within the literature circle. The group meets regularly to discuss the text, sharing their thoughts and insights with one another, and building upon each other's ideas. The teacher takes a backseat role, serving as a facilitator, while the students take ownership of the discussion.

During a literature circle meeting, students take on specific roles, such as discussion director, summarizer, vocabulary enricher, and connector. These roles encourage students to engage with the text in different ways and take responsibility for their own learning. Students learn from each other through the sharing of their ideas and perspectives, and they develop their critical thinking skills by questioning and challenging each other's interpretations of the text.

Research has shown that literature circles have a positive impact on student engagement, motivation, and reading achievement. They provide opportunities for students to develop critical thinking skills, improve their communication skills, and increase their knowledge of literature. By participating in literature circles, students can also build social connections with their peers and feel a sense of belonging in the classroom.

Benefits of Literature Circles

IN THIS SECTION, WE will explore the many benefits of literature circles in the classroom. Literature circles have been shown to have numerous benefits for students, teachers, and the classroom community as a whole.

Benefits to Students

One of the biggest benefits of literature circles is that they promote active and engaged reading. When students are reading as part of a literature circle, they are not simply reading for comprehension or to complete an assignment. Instead, they are reading for understanding, interpretation, and discussion. This type of reading encourages students to take ownership of their learning and to develop critical thinking skills.

Literature circles also provide opportunities for students to practice important social skills, such as active listening, effective communication, and collaboration. As students work together to discuss the text, they learn to share their ideas and to respectfully listen to the ideas of others. These skills are valuable both inside and outside of the classroom.

Another benefit of literature circles is that they allow for differentiation in the classroom. Since students are often working in groups, they can be grouped according to their reading level or interests. This allows for a more personalized approach to reading instruction and can help students to feel more invested in their learning.

Benefits to Teachers

While literature circles require careful planning and preparation, they can actually save teachers time in the long run. By allowing students to take ownership of their learning, teachers can spend less time lecturing and more time facilitating meaningful discussions. Additionally, since literature circles often involve students working in groups, teachers can circulate the room and provide targeted support as needed.

Another benefit of literature circles is that they can help teachers to identify areas where students are struggling. As students work through the text and participate in discussions, teachers can observe their progress and identify areas where they may need additional support.

Benefits to the Classroom Community

Finally, literature circles can help to create a sense of community in the classroom. By working together in small groups, students develop relationships and learn to support each other. Additionally, literature circles can provide opportunities for students to share their backgrounds, experiences, and perspectives, which can help to create a more inclusive and welcoming classroom environment.

Overall, literature circles are a valuable tool for promoting active and engaged reading, developing critical thinking and social skills, providing differentiation in the classroom, saving teachers time, identifying areas where students need support, and creating a sense of community in the classroom.

Promoting Student Engagement and Motivation

STUDENT ENGAGEMENT and motivation are crucial components of successful learning, and literature circles are a powerful tool for promoting engagement and motivation among students. Below are just some of the ways in which literature circles have been shown to increase student engagement and motivation:

Increased Student Participation

One of the most significant benefits of literature circles is the increased participation and engagement of students. In literature circles, students have the opportunity to work together and share their thoughts and ideas about the text they are reading. This sharing and collaboration lead to increased participation and engagement, as students become invested in the discussions and debates that arise.

Personalized Learning

Another benefit of literature circles is the personalized learning experience they provide. Literature circles allow students to explore topics and themes that are of interest to them, which can lead to a more personalized learning experience. Students are more likely to be engaged and motivated when they have a personal connection to the material they are learning.

Enhanced Critical Thinking

Literature circles also promote critical thinking skills among students. As students discuss the text, they are required to analyze and interpret the material, developing critical thinking skills that will benefit them in other areas of their academic and personal lives.

Increased Student Confidence

As students participate in literature circles, they are given the opportunity to share their thoughts and ideas with their peers. This sharing and collaboration can lead to increased confidence among students, as they learn to express their opinions and ideas in a supportive environment.

Improved Social Skills

Finally, literature circles promote improved social skills among students. As students work together, they learn to communicate effectively, listen actively, and respect the opinions of others. These skills will benefit students both inside and outside of the classroom.

Different Types of Literature Circles

THERE ARE DIFFERENT types of literature circles that can be implemented in the classroom. The type of literature circle to be used depends on various factors such as student age range, subject, and the teacher's preference. This section will provide a brief description of the different types of literature circles that can be used in the classroom.

Traditional Literature Circles

Traditional literature circles are the most common type of literature circles. They are typically used in language arts classrooms and are best suited for middle and high school students. In traditional literature circles, students read the same book and then discuss it in groups. Each student is assigned a specific role such as discussion director, summarizer, illustrator, etc.

Multigenre Literature Circles

Multigenre literature circles are another type of literature circle that can be used in the classroom. In this type of literature circle, students read several books or texts on a similar topic and discuss them in groups. The focus is on exploring different genres such as poetry, non-fiction, fiction, and drama. Multigenre literature circles can be used for all grade levels and can be adapted to different subjects.

Book Clubs

Book clubs are another type of literature circle that can be used in the classroom. In this type of literature circle, students read a book of their choice and then discuss it in groups. The focus is on personal choice and reflection. Book clubs are best suited for upper elementary, middle, and high school students.

Genre Study

In genre study literature circles, students explore a particular genre such as mystery, science fiction, or fantasy. They read different books or texts in the chosen genre and then discuss them in groups. This type of literature circle is best suited for upper elementary and middle school students.

Content Area Literature Circles

Content area literature circles are used to explore a specific content area such as social studies or science. Students read different texts related to the content area and then discuss them in groups. This type of literature circle is best suited for middle and high school students.

Setting Up Literature Circles

I REMEMBER THE TIME when my literature circle group was having a hard time getting along and staying on track during our discussions. We all had different opinions and it seemed like we couldn't find any common ground. I was starting to get frustrated because I felt like we were wasting our time and not really learning anything.

Luckily, our teacher noticed that our group was struggling and stepped in to help us out. She started by asking us questions that forced us to think more deeply about the book and how it related to our own lives. She also encouraged us to listen to each other's perspectives and find ways to build on them, rather than just dismissing them outright.

At first, it was still a bit difficult to get everyone on the same page, but our teacher kept pushing us to think and engage in respectful dialogue. Eventually, we started to understand each other's perspectives more and find ways to build on each other's ideas.

Without our teacher's help, I don't think our group would have been able to overcome our differences and have productive discussions. I learned the importance of being patient and willing to listen to others, even if their opinions are different from my own.

Literature circles are a great way to encourage students to read, analyze, and discuss a variety of texts in a collaborative and student-centered way. But how do you set up literature circles in the classroom? This section provides a step-by-step guide on how to set up a literature circle that promotes student engagement, encourages critical thinking, and provides opportunities for meaningful discussions.

Step 1: Choose the Text(s)

The first step in setting up a literature circle is choosing the text(s). This can be a novel, short stories, articles, poems, or even film. It is important to choose a text that is age-appropriate and that aligns with the learning objectives for the class. When it comes to literature circles, the texts being read are at the core of the entire process. Therefore, it is important for teachers to choose texts that will be engaging, appropriate, and meaningful to their students. There are a number of factors that teachers should consider when selecting texts for literature circles, and these are explored in more detail in a later section.

Several key factors to consider when choosing texts are: student interests, reading level, diversity and representation, relevance to curriculum, and accessibility. By taking these factors into consideration, teachers can choose texts that will engage and motivate their students, while also promoting critical thinking, empathy, and an appreciation for literature.

Step 2: Determine the Number of Groups and Group Size

Next, decide on the number of groups and group size. This will depend on the number of students in the class and the size of the text(s). It is important to have groups that are small enough to ensure that every student has a chance to participate and contribute to the discussion. When implementing literature circles in the classroom, the number of groups and group size are critical factors to consider. Here are some factors to keep in mind:

- **Classroom size:** Consider the total number of students in the classroom, and ensure that each student is placed in a group. Also, think about the classroom space and the number of discussion groups that can take place simultaneously.

- **Text complexity:** The complexity of the text can affect the number of groups and their size. For example, if the text is challenging, it may be better to have smaller groups, so students have more opportunities to share their understanding of the text. Conversely, if the text is less complex, larger groups can be formed.

- **Student needs:** Consider the individual needs of each student, including their reading level, language proficiency, and academic goals. If students have similar needs, they can be grouped together to provide more focused instruction.

- **Time constraints:** Consider the amount of time available for literature circles. If time is limited, it may be better to form larger groups to ensure that each student has a chance to participate in the discussion.

- **Group dynamics:** Think about the group dynamics when forming groups. Students who work well together and complement each other's strengths and weaknesses can be placed in a group to promote a more productive discussion.

In terms of group size, there are pros and cons to both large and small groups. Smaller groups can lead to more in-depth discussions and give each student more opportunities to participate. However, larger groups provide more diverse perspectives and can lead to a more dynamic discussion. As a general rule, groups of four to six students are ideal for literature circles.

Ultimately, the decision on the number of groups and group size should be based on the specific needs of the students and the goals of the literature circle. Teachers should be flexible and willing to adjust group size and number as necessary to meet the needs of their students.

Step 3: Assign Roles

Assign roles to each member of the literature circle. Some common roles include discussion leader, summarizer, connector, vocabulary master, and illustrator. These roles help to ensure that every student has a specific responsibility and that the discussion is well-structured. In order to maximize student engagement and learning during literature circles, it is important for teachers to assign roles to students. Each role is designed to encourage active participation and to ensure that students are comprehending and analyzing the text at a deeper level. Assigning roles in literature circles allows students to take ownership of their learning and encourages them to collaborate with their peers.

The benefits of assigning roles in literature circles are numerous. It ensures that every student has a specific task to focus on, which helps to prevent boredom and disengagement. Furthermore, it ensures that all students have a chance to contribute to the discussion and that no one student dominates the conversation. By assigning specific roles, the teacher can also ensure that all aspects of the text are explored and that students are exposed to a variety of critical thinking skills.

It is important for teachers to carefully consider the roles they assign to students. They should be designed to challenge students and to encourage them to think critically about the text. Roles should be assigned based on the strengths and interests of individual students and should be varied enough to ensure that each student has the opportunity to develop a range of skills.

In another section later in this chapter, we will provide detailed examples of the types of roles that can be assigned in literature circles. These roles include discussion director, literary luminary, summarizer, connector, vocabulary enricher, and illustrator. By assigning these roles, teachers can create a collaborative learning environment that promotes engagement, active participation, and critical thinking.

Step 4: Set a Schedule

Create a schedule for the literature circle meetings. It is important to establish a consistent meeting time and place. Additionally, consider the length of the text and the number of meetings needed to complete the text. In literature circles, setting a schedule is crucial for the success of the activity. A clear and consistent schedule helps students develop a routine and ensures that all groups have an equal amount of time to discuss the book.

Step 5: Establish Guidelines for Discussions

Guidelines for discussions include norms for participation, active listening, and respectful communication. Encourage students to challenge each other's ideas respectfully and to build on each other's contributions. Establishing guidelines for discussions is crucial to ensure that students have a productive and safe space to share their thoughts and ideas. These guidelines serve as expectations for how students should interact with each other during literature circle meetings.

It is important to establish guidelines for respectful communication. Students should be reminded to speak respectfully and listen actively to their peers. They should also be encouraged to ask clarifying questions and to provide evidence to support their ideas.

Guidelines for participation should be established. This may include expectations for attendance and punctuality, as well as guidelines for how much each student should contribute to the discussion. It is important to encourage all students to participate, but also to avoid dominating the discussion.

Guidelines for confidentiality should be discussed. Students should be reminded that what is said in literature circles should stay within the group and that personal experiences shared during discussions should be respected and not shared with others outside of the group.

Guidelines for handling disagreements should be established. Students should be encouraged to respectfully disagree with their peers and to share their own perspectives without attacking others. They should also be taught how to respectfully acknowledge and respond to differing viewpoints.

It is important to establish guidelines for the use of technology during literature circle meetings. This may include guidelines for the use of phones, tablets, or laptops during discussions to ensure that students remain engaged with the text and their peers.

By establishing clear guidelines for discussions, teachers can create a safe and productive environment for students to engage in literature circles. These guidelines will help to promote respectful communication, active participation, confidentiality, handling disagreements, and responsible use of technology.

Step 6: Monitor and Facilitate

Finally, as the teacher, it is important to monitor and facilitate the literature circles. Check in with the groups regularly to make sure they are on track and to offer support and guidance as needed. Provide feedback on the discussions and individual contributions to the group. Monitoring and facilitating are critical components of literature circles that allow teachers to assess student learning, support student engagement, and ensure the success of the activity.

When students are participating in literature circles, teachers must monitor the discussions to ensure that the groups are staying on task and that all students are contributing to the conversation. This can be done by walking around the room and listening in on conversations, taking notes, and keeping track of the progress of each group.

Facilitating involves guiding the discussion and helping students stay focused on the text while promoting critical thinking and analysis. This can involve asking open-ended questions, clarifying confusion, and encouraging students to build on one another's ideas.

Facilitating also involves ensuring that all students have an opportunity to contribute to the conversation. Teachers can help quieter students participate by prompting them with questions, providing sentence stems, and encouraging them to share their thoughts.

Monitoring and facilitating are important because they allow teachers to evaluate student learning and provide support where needed. By monitoring the conversations, teachers can assess whether students are grasping the key concepts of the text and identify areas where they may need additional instruction. Facilitating the discussion also promotes critical thinking and analysis, helping students to deepen their understanding of the text and develop their analytical skills.

Choosing Appropriate Texts

CHOOSING TEXTS FOR a literature circle is an important step in ensuring a successful and engaging experience for students. There are several factors to consider when selecting texts for a literature circle, including student interest, complexity, relevance, and diversity.

First and foremost, it is important to choose texts that are interesting and engaging to students. Teachers can survey students or ask for their input to determine what genres, topics, or authors they are most interested in. This can help ensure that students are invested in the reading process and are more likely to participate in discussions.

Another important factor to consider is the complexity of the text. The chosen text should be challenging enough to promote critical thinking and analysis but not so difficult that it discourages students from reading or participating. It is important to consider the reading level of the students and select texts that are appropriate for their age and skill level.

Relevance is also an important factor to consider when selecting texts for a literature circle. The chosen text should be relevant to the students' lives and experiences, and should address themes and topics that are important to them. This can help students connect with the text on a personal level and engage more deeply with the material.

Another factor to consider when choosing texts is the number of texts each group will read. Typically, literature circles involve students reading multiple texts over a period of time, with each group reading a different text. The number of texts each group reads depends on several factors, including the length of the texts, the complexity of the texts, and the amount of time available for the literature circle. A good rule of thumb is to choose three to four texts for each group to read.

It's also important to consider the literary elements present in each text. Literature circles are designed to promote critical thinking and analysis, so texts should be chosen that provide opportunities for these skills to be developed. For example, a mystery novel might be chosen for a group that is interested in analyzing plot and character development, while a historical fiction novel might be chosen for a group that is interested in examining historical context and perspective.

It is important to choose texts that are diverse and inclusive. Literature circles provide an opportunity to expose students to different perspectives and experiences, and selecting texts that represent a range of cultures, races, genders, and abilities can help promote empathy and understanding.

Finally, when choosing texts for literature circles, it's important to keep in mind any curricular or state standards that need to be met. Texts should align with learning objectives and support student growth in specific areas.

Forming Groups and Assigning Roles

CREATING STUDENT GROUPS for literature circles and assigning roles are two important decisions that teachers must make when implementing this instructional approach. The following are some factors that should be considered:

Creating Student Groups

- **Reading Level:** Teachers should group students based on their reading level to ensure that all students have access to the text and can participate in discussions. This helps to prevent frustration and confusion for struggling readers and boredom for advanced readers.

- **Learning Styles:** Teachers should also consider students' learning styles when creating groups. For example, if a student is an auditory learner, they may benefit from being in a group where discussion is the primary method of learning.

- **Personality and Interests**: Teachers should also take into consideration students' personalities and interests when creating groups. This can help to foster positive group dynamics and increase engagement.

Assigning Roles

The purpose of assigning roles in literature circles is to give students specific responsibilities during group discussions and to hold them accountable for their learning. When assigning roles, teachers should consider the following:

- **Student Strengths:** Assign roles based on students' strengths and interests. For example, a student who loves to draw may enjoy the role of illustrator.

- **Balanced Workload:** Assign roles fairly, so that each student has an equal opportunity to participate in discussions and contribute to the group's learning.

- **Rotation:** Consider rotating roles so that students have the opportunity to try different roles throughout the literature circle process.

In addition, teachers should communicate the purpose and expectations of each role clearly to students so that they understand their responsibilities and can prepare for group discussions accordingly. The next section provides a list of commonly-used roles along with a brief description.

Common Literature Circle Roles

THERE IS NO PRESCRIPTIVE list of recommended roles. Teachers are encouraged to create and select roles based on the needs of their class with the goal of maximizing student participation and engagement.

Discussion Director

Responsible for creating a list of open-ended questions that promote critical thinking and discussion about the assigned reading. The Discussion Director should also facilitate the discussion and ensure that everyone has an opportunity to contribute.

Literary Luminary

Responsible for choosing a passage from the reading that they found particularly interesting, thought-provoking, or well-written. The Literary Luminary should read the passage aloud to the group and explain why they chose it.

Word Wizard

Responsible for identifying and defining challenging vocabulary words in the reading. The Word Wizard should also provide examples of how these words are used in context.

Connector

Responsible for making connections between the reading and other texts, personal experiences, or current events. The Connector should help the group to see how the themes and ideas in the reading relate to their own lives and the world around them.

Illustrator

Responsible for creating visual representations of scenes or characters from the reading. The Illustrator should share their artwork with the group and explain why they chose to depict certain elements in a particular way.

Summarizer

Responsible for providing a brief summary of the assigned reading. The Summarizer should also help the group to stay on track and ensure that everyone understands the main ideas and events of the story.

Researcher

Responsible for conducting background research on the author, historical events or cultural references mentioned in the reading, and presenting this information to the group. The Researcher should also help the group to understand the context in which the reading was written and how it may have influenced the author's writing.

Strategies for Managing Literature Circles

EFFECTIVE MANAGEMENT of literature circles is essential to ensure that students are on-task and engaged in productive discussions. Here are some effective strategies that teachers can use to manage lit circles in the classroom:

Establish Clear Guidelines

Before starting the literature circle, teachers should establish clear guidelines for group meetings. This includes expectations for how groups will be formed, how often they will meet, how much reading should be done in between meetings, and how group discussions should be conducted. By establishing clear expectations from the outset, teachers can help to ensure that students are prepared and ready to participate in literature circles. These guidelines should include expectations for group members, such as taking turns, listening actively, and showing respect for one another.

Monitor And Facilitate Discussions

Teachers should monitor group discussions to ensure that they are on task and that all group members are participating. They can also facilitate discussions by asking thought-provoking questions and encouraging students to explore different perspectives.

Use a Checklist

Another strategy for managing literature circles is to use a checklist to keep track of student progress. A checklist can help teachers to ensure that all group members are contributing to discussions. Teachers can use the checklist to keep track of the books that each group is reading, the roles that each student is assigned, and any other tasks that need to be completed in order to prepare for group discussions.

Use A Timer

Using a timer can help keep students on task and ensure that all group members have an equal amount of time to share their ideas and insights.

Provide Time for Reflection

Reflection is an important component of the literature circle process. Teachers should provide students with time to reflect on what they have read and learned, and to think about how they can apply this knowledge to other areas of their lives. Teachers can provide time for reflection through journaling or other writing activities, or through class discussions.

Assign Group Roles

Assigning roles within each literature circle group can help to promote accountability and ensure that all students are actively participating in discussions.

Use technology

Teachers can use technology tools such as Google Classroom or Edmodo to manage literature circles. These tools allow teachers to monitor group discussions, share resources, and communicate with students outside of class.

Encourage Collaboration

Encouraging collaboration between literature circle groups can help to foster a sense of community within the classroom. Teachers can encourage collaboration by having groups share their findings with one another, or by having groups work together on projects or presentations related to the books that they have read.

Provide feedback

Teachers should provide regular feedback to students on their participation and contributions to the literature circle. This feedback can be used to guide future discussions and help students improve their communication skills.

Offer choice

To increase student engagement, teachers can offer choice in the selection of texts or roles. This allows students to have some control over their learning and can help them to feel more invested in the literature circle.

Teaching Strategies for Literature Circles

WHEN I FIRST HEARD about the literature circle assignment, I was scared. English is not my first language, and sometimes reading is hard for me. But as we began reading the book together in our group, I felt supported and more confident in my abilities.

One of the biggest challenges I face when reading by myself is understanding new vocabulary words or phrases that are unfamiliar to me. In our literature circle, however, we were able to discuss and clarify unfamiliar words or concepts together. My group members would explain and give examples, which helped me to better understand the text. I also found it helpful when the teacher provided a list of vocabulary words and their definitions before we started reading.

Another benefit of the literature circle was the opportunity to practice speaking English. I sometimes struggle with speaking in class because I am not always confident in my pronunciation or grammar. However, in the literature circle, I felt more comfortable speaking because I knew my group members were supportive and non-judgmental. It was also helpful when the teacher encouraged us to use sentence stems or provided prompts to guide our discussions.

Overall, I am grateful for the experience of participating in a literature circle. It helped me to better understand the text, build my confidence in speaking English, and feel supported by my group members and teacher.

There are several strategies that teachers can use to teach literature circles effectively.

Model Discussions

Before students start their literature circles, it can be helpful for the teacher to model what a good discussion looks like. This can involve demonstrating how to ask open-ended questions, how to respond to others, and how to respectfully disagree. Teachers play an important role in modeling effective discussions for literature circles. Modeling discussions provides students with a clear understanding of the expectations for participation and helps them develop the skills needed to engage in meaningful conversations about literature.

- **Demonstrate Active Listening:** Teachers should model active listening by making eye contact with the speaker, nodding to show understanding, and asking follow-up questions to clarify or expand on ideas.

- **Use Open-Ended Questions:** Teachers can model effective discussion techniques by asking open-ended questions that encourage deeper thinking and discussion. These types of questions can help students connect the text to their own experiences and worldviews.

- **Encourage Multiple Perspectives:** Model how to respectfully disagree with others and share multiple perspectives. Encouraging students to share diverse perspectives can lead to more thoughtful and nuanced discussions.

- **Provide Feedback:** Teachers should model how to provide constructive feedback to other students in the group. This includes pointing out strengths, asking questions to help clarify ideas, and making suggestions for improvement.

- **Share Personal Connections:** Teachers can model how to make personal connections to the text by sharing their own experiences, thoughts, and feelings about the literature. This can help students feel more comfortable sharing their own personal connections.

Teach Discussion Skills

It's important to explicitly teach students the skills they need to participate in effective discussions. This can involve teaching them how to listen actively, how to paraphrase what others say, and how to make connections between the text and their own experiences. Explicitly teaching discussion skills is crucial for the success of literature circles. Some students may come to the table with strong discussion skills, while others may need more guidance and practice.

- **Identify Key Discussion Skills:** Teachers should identify key discussion skills that students need to be successful in literature circles. These may include active listening, making connections, asking open-ended questions, supporting opinions with evidence, and more. Teachers should then explicitly teach and model each skill.

- **Provide Examples:** Teachers should provide examples of effective discussion skills in action. This could include examples from literature circles or real-life discussions. Teachers can then lead a discussion with students to analyze and discuss what makes these examples effective.

- **Practice In Small Groups:** Before diving into full literature circle discussions, teachers can provide opportunities for students to practice their discussion skills in smaller groups. This could involve discussing short articles or excerpts from a text. This allows for more individualized feedback and allows students to practice their skills in a lower-stakes environment.

- **Use Discussion Prompts:** Teachers can provide discussion prompts to guide students in their discussions and ensure they are hitting on the key skills. These prompts can be open-ended questions, quotes from the text, or guiding themes.

- **Peer Feedback:** After a discussion, students can provide feedback to their peers on their discussion skills. This not only provides valuable feedback but also helps to reinforce the importance of strong discussion skills.

- **Reflect And Revise:** This could involve individual reflections, group reflections, or even whole-class discussions. Teachers can then use this feedback to guide their instruction and ensure students are developing their discussion skills throughout the literature circle experience.

Scaffold The Reading

Teachers can help students prepare for their literature circles by scaffolding the reading process. This can involve breaking the text into manageable chunks, providing guiding questions, and using graphic organizers to help students make sense of the text. Scaffolding is a key component of literature circles, as it can help students to better understand the text and engage in more meaningful discussions. There are several ways that teachers can scaffold the reading process for their students.

- **Pre-Reading Activities:** Before starting the reading, teachers can introduce the text and its context through various activities, such as providing background information, exploring key vocabulary, or generating questions based on the title and cover.

- **Guiding Questions:** During the reading process, teachers can provide students with guiding questions to help them focus on important elements of the text, such as characters, themes, and literary devices. These questions can also be used to encourage critical thinking and deeper analysis of the text.

- **Graphic Organizers:** Teachers can provide students with graphic organizers, such as story maps or character charts, to help them organize their thoughts and better understand the relationships between different elements of the text.

- **Close Reading:** Teachers can guide students through the process of close reading, in which they analyze the text at a deep level, looking for specific details and evidence to support their interpretations. This can be done through a guided reading activity or through independent work.

- **Annotation:** Teachers can encourage students to annotate the text as they read, highlighting key passages, making notes, and asking questions. This can help students to stay engaged with the text and develop their own ideas and interpretations.

- **Discussion Preparation:** Prior to the literature circle discussion, teachers can provide students with specific tasks or questions to prepare them for the discussion. This can include analyzing a particular aspect of the text, summarizing key events, or generating discussion questions.

Provide Feedback

Teachers should provide feedback to students on their participation in the literature circle. This can involve providing written feedback on discussion skills, or providing individual conferences to discuss students' progress. Providing feedback is an important component of any effective teaching practice, and it is no different for literature circles. Feedback can take many forms, and teachers should consider the benefits and drawbacks of each when providing feedback to students in literature circles.

- **Written Feedback:** Written feedback allows students to review and reflect on the feedback at their own pace, and it can also serve as a record of progress over time. However, written feedback can sometimes be overwhelming, and students may struggle to understand and apply the feedback.

- **Verbal Feedback:** Verbal feedback can be tailored to the specific needs of the student, and it allows for immediate clarification or follow-up questions. However, verbal feedback can sometimes be forgotten or misinterpreted by the student, and it can be difficult to remember specific feedback over time.

- **Peer Feedback:** Peer feedback allows students to practice critical thinking and communication skills. However, peer feedback can sometimes be too general or not specific enough, and students may struggle with providing constructive criticism.

- **Self-Reflection:** Self-reflection encourages students to take ownership of their learning and helps to build self-awareness and metacognition skills. However, self-reflection can sometimes be too general or too critical, and students may struggle to accurately evaluate their own progress.

Encourage Reflection

After the literature circle has ended, it can be helpful to encourage students to reflect on their experience. This can involve asking them to write about what they learned, what they found challenging, and what they enjoyed about the literature circle. This can help students understand their own learning process and identify areas for growth. Reflecting on their literature circle experience is an important component of the learning process for students. It helps them to think critically about their learning and gain a better understanding of the material they read.

- **Journaling:** Students can write about their thoughts, feelings, and opinions on the material they read, as well as their experience with the literature circle process. This method is beneficial because it allows students to reflect privately, which can be helpful for more introspective students. It also helps students to process their thoughts and feelings in a structured way, which can improve their communication skills.

- **Group Discussion:** This can be done as a whole class discussion or within their individual groups. Group discussion is beneficial because it allows students to hear other perspectives and opinions on the material they read. It also helps students to practice their communication skills, particularly in terms of active listening and responding to others.

- **Exit Slips:** Students write down their thoughts and feelings on a slip of paper, which they then hand in to the teacher. This method is beneficial because it allows for a quick and easy way for students to reflect on their learning. It also helps teachers to assess student understanding and address any concerns or questions students may have.

- **Digital Tools:** Digital tools such as blogs, discussion forums, and online journals can also be used for reflection. This method is beneficial because it allows for more flexibility in terms of when and where students can reflect. It also provides students with a way to share their reflections with a wider audience, which can be motivating for some students.

- **Creative Projects:** Art, music, and drama can be used as a reflection method. This method is beneficial because it allows for more creativity and personal expression in the reflection process. It can also be helpful for students who may struggle with traditional forms of reflection.

Role of the Teacher in Literature Circles

THE ROLE OF THE TEACHER in literature circles is essential to the success of the activity. The teacher should provide guidance, support, and feedback throughout the process.

Facilitator

The teacher should facilitate the literature circle discussions by providing structure and guidance. This includes establishing discussion guidelines, monitoring the discussions, and helping students stay on task.

Model

The teacher should model effective discussion techniques by participating in the literature circle discussions. This helps to demonstrate to students the types of questions and comments that are productive for the discussion.

Scaffolder

The teacher should scaffold the reading process by providing background knowledge, vocabulary, and comprehension support before and during the literature circle discussions. This can include previewing the text, providing graphic organizers, and offering guidance on how to annotate texts.

Evaluator

The teacher should evaluate student performance throughout the literature circle process. This includes assessing participation in the discussion, evaluating the quality of student questions and comments, and providing feedback on student performance.

Coach

The teacher should coach students on how to improve their discussion skills. This includes offering suggestions for how to ask better questions, how to make insightful comments, and how to respond thoughtfully to others' comments.

Resource Provider

The teacher should provide resources to support the literature circle process. This includes providing a variety of texts for students to choose from, creating discussion prompts, and offering materials to support the reading process (such as audio recordings or visual aids).

Differentiated Instruction in Literature Circles

DIFFERENTIATION IN literature circles refers to the process of providing students with varied learning experiences that match their individual needs and abilities. As such, teachers need to consider the different aspects of differentiation to ensure that all students are actively engaged, challenged, and supported. Here are some ways that teachers can differentiate instruction in literature circles:

Texts

One of the primary ways to differentiate literature circles is by selecting texts that are appropriate for the different reading levels and interests of the students in the class. Teachers may consider assigning different texts to different groups based on students' reading level, interests, and abilities.

Grouping

Grouping students in literature circles is another way to differentiate instruction. Teachers may form groups based on shared interests, reading levels, or learning styles. Additionally, teachers may consider assigning different roles to each group member based on their strengths, interests, or learning needs.

Role Assignments

Assigning roles is an excellent way to differentiate instruction in literature circles. Teachers can provide students with different role options, such as summarizer, discussion leader, literary luminary, or connector, and allow students to select the role that best matches their strengths and interests.

Scaffolding

Teachers can differentiate instruction by providing different levels of scaffolding for students. For example, struggling readers may receive more guidance or support in the form of pre-reading activities, graphic organizers, or reading aids. Advanced readers, on the other hand, may be given more challenging texts or tasks to complete.

Assessments

Teachers may differentiate instruction in literature circles by providing different types of assessments that align with students' individual needs and abilities. For example, teachers can provide varied options for students to demonstrate their understanding, such as written responses, oral presentations, or multimedia projects.

Teacher Support

Finally, teachers play an essential role in supporting student learning and differentiation in literature circles. Teachers may provide individualized feedback, ongoing support, and opportunities for one-on-one conferences to help students succeed in their literature circle roles. Teachers may also provide targeted instruction or small group lessons to support struggling learners or challenge advanced learners.

Options Beyond Books for Literature Circles

I USED TO THINK READING was boring. I was never interested in picking up a book or even trying to read it. So, when my teacher told me we were going to participate in literature circles, I didn't get why everybody else was all excited. I thought it was going to be another experience where I was bored stiff.

However, my teacher decided to include a movie as one of the texts we could choose from. I was really surprised by this because I didn't think my teacher would allow us to watch a movie instead of reading a book. It seemed like cheating in a way. Anyway, we watched the movie in class and then discussed it in our group. I was surprised at how much I enjoyed talking about the movie and hearing what my classmates had to say.

I decided to try reading one of the books as well, and I found that I enjoyed it more than I thought I would. It was still a bit difficult for me, but with the support of my group members and teacher, I was able to understand it better.

What Are Non-Traditional Texts?

NON-TRADITIONAL TEXTS refer to any kind of text that is not a traditional, print-based narrative or informational text. While novels, short stories, and nonfiction books are commonly used in literature circles and other reading-based activities in the classroom, non-traditional texts include a variety of other media such as films, podcasts, graphic novels, poetry, music lyrics, and more.

The use of non-traditional texts in the classroom is becoming increasingly popular as educators recognize that they can offer unique benefits for students. Non-traditional texts can help engage students who may struggle with traditional text formats, as well as offer new perspectives and ways of interpreting information. For example, a film can provide visual and auditory support to aid comprehension, while a graphic novel can provide a new level of engagement for visual learners.

Additionally, non-traditional texts can expose students to different genres and forms of expression that may not be included in traditional reading lists. This can help broaden students' cultural understanding and encourage critical thinking about media and its impact on society.

Benefits of Using Non-Traditional Texts

INCLUDING NON-TRADITIONAL texts in literature circles can provide a wealth of benefits for students. For one, it can help engage students who may struggle with traditional texts, such as struggling readers or English language learners. Non-traditional texts can provide a fresh perspective and can be more relatable to students, as they often cover contemporary issues and current events.

Additionally, non-traditional texts can help promote critical thinking and media literacy skills. For example, including film in literature circles can encourage students to analyze the use of camera angles, lighting, and sound in order to better understand the story and its themes. Similarly, including graphic novels can help students analyze the use of visuals and the integration of text and image to convey meaning.

Another benefit of incorporating non-traditional texts is that it can help students develop skills that are valuable in today's society. For example, analyzing and interpreting media is an important skill for navigating the complex media landscape in which we live. Including non-traditional texts in literature circles can help students develop these skills and become more informed and critical consumers of media.

Examples of Non-Traditional Texts

NON-TRADITIONAL TEXT options can be a great way to spice up literature circles and engage students who may not be as excited about reading traditional texts. Here are several options to consider:

Graphic Novels

Graphic novels are a great option for visual learners or students who struggle with traditional novels. They can also provide a unique way to approach complex themes and ideas.

Poetry

Poetry can be an excellent option for literature circles, as it encourages close reading and analysis. Poems are often shorter than traditional novels, so they can also be a good option for struggling readers.

Short Stories

Like poetry, short stories can be an excellent option for struggling readers or students who may not have as much time to devote to longer novels. They can also be a great way to expose students to different authors and writing styles.

Plays

Plays are a fantastic option for literature circles, as they encourage students to read aloud and think about the performance aspect of literature. They can also provide an opportunity for students to explore different genres, from classic Shakespeare to contemporary plays.

Film

Film can be an excellent option for literature circles, especially for students who may be more visually oriented or struggle with traditional texts. Teachers can choose films based on books, plays, or other texts, and then have students compare and contrast the two versions.

Each of these non-traditional text options has its own unique strengths and benefits. Graphic novels and poetry, for example, can be great for visual and analytical learners, while short stories and plays can be better for struggling readers or those with limited time. Film can also provide a unique way for students to engage with texts and think about adaptation and interpretation. Teachers can choose the option that best fits the needs and interests of their students.

Incorporating Non-Traditional Texts into Literature Circles

INCORPORATING NON-TRADITIONAL texts, such as films, graphic novels, or podcasts, can add variety and interest to literature circles. Here are two approaches for incorporating non-traditional texts into lit circles:

Thematic approach

Choose a theme and select traditional and non-traditional texts that fit the theme. For example, if the theme is "coming of age," the traditional text could be The Catcher in the Rye by J.D. Salinger, and the non-traditional text could be the film The Perks of Being a Wallflower directed by Stephen Chbosky. Students can read/watch the texts and discuss how the characters in each text experience coming of age. This approach allows for diverse perspectives and allows students to explore the theme through multiple mediums.

Parallel approach

Choose a traditional text and pair it with a non-traditional text that has a similar theme or message. For example, if the traditional text is To Kill a Mockingbird by Harper Lee, the non-traditional text could be the film A Time to Kill directed by Joel Schumacher. Both texts deal with themes of racism and social injustice. Students can compare and contrast the treatment of the themes in each text and consider how the different mediums affect their understanding of the themes.

When incorporating non-traditional texts, it is important to consider the unique features of the text and how it may require different approaches to reading and discussion. For example, a graphic novel may require students to consider the visual elements in addition to the text, while a film may require close attention to visual and auditory cues. Teachers should provide guidance and support to students in navigating these different mediums. Additionally, providing multiple options for non-traditional texts allows for differentiation and allows students of differing abilities to choose a text that best suits their learning style and interests.

Assigned roles can be similar and different when incorporating non-traditional texts into lit circles. The main similarity is that assigned roles still serve the same purpose of promoting engagement, discussion, and critical thinking among group members. However, the specific roles may differ depending on the type of non-traditional text being used. For example, when using a film, roles such as "cinematographer" or "sound designer" may be assigned to students to analyze the technical aspects of the film, while roles such as "character analyst" or "theme tracker" may be assigned to students to analyze the narrative elements.

In addition, the methods for fulfilling assigned roles may also differ. For example, when using a podcast as a non-traditional text, students may be assigned roles such as "host," "guest," or "fact-checker," and may be expected to produce their own content or conduct interviews related to the podcast. On the other hand, when using a graphic novel, students may be assigned roles such as "visual analyst" or "panel decoder," and may be expected to analyze the visual aspects of the text.

Regardless of the specific roles or methods, the purpose of assigned roles in incorporating non-traditional texts into lit circles remains the same: to provide students with a structured framework for analyzing and discussing the text, and to promote active participation and engagement among all group members.

Variations on Student Roles for Non-Traditional Texts

AS WITH MORE TRADITIONAL literature circles, there is no set list of roles for engaging with non-traditional texts. The two lists below are samples of commonly used roles, but teachers are encouraged to innovate and create roles that work for their students.

Graphic Novel Literature Circle Roles

Discussion Director

The Discussion Director could prepare questions for group discussion before reading the graphic novel, focusing on elements such as plot, character, setting, and theme. After reading the graphic novel, the Discussion Director could lead the group in a discussion of these questions, encouraging members to reflect on how the graphic novel conveyed its message through visual and textual means.

Literary Luminary

The Literary Luminary could identify key panels or pages in the graphic novel that were particularly striking, moving, or memorable, and share these with the group. They could discuss how these moments contributed to the overall meaning or message of the graphic novel.

Connector

The Connector could research the graphic novel's author, illustrator, or publisher, and share information about their backgrounds, influences, and other works. They could also connect the graphic novel to other works of literature or art that address similar themes or issues.

Investigator

The Investigator could research the historical or cultural context in which the graphic novel was made, and share information about relevant events, social movements, or political issues. They could also discuss how the graphic novel reflects or comments on these events or issues.

Artist

The Artist could analyze the graphic novel's visual elements, such as panel layout, composition, and style. They could discuss how these elements contribute to the overall atmosphere or meaning of the graphic novel.

Word Wizard

Responsible for identifying and defining challenging vocabulary words in the reading. The Word Wizard should also provide examples of how these words are used in context. They could explain how the visual elements help with creating meaning from the challenging words.

Historian

The Historian could research the history of graphic novels and comics as a medium and discuss how the graphic novel fits into this history. They could also investigate how the graphic novel's style, techniques, or themes have influenced other graphic novels or media.

FILM LITERATURE CIRCLE Roles

Discussion Director

The Discussion Director could prepare questions for group discussion before viewing the film, focusing on elements such as plot, character, setting, and theme. After the film, the Discussion Director could lead the group in a discussion of these questions, encouraging members to reflect on how the film conveyed its message through visual and auditory means.

Literary Luminary

The Literary Luminary could identify key moments in the film that were particularly striking, moving, or memorable, and share these moments with the group. They could discuss how these moments contributed to the overall meaning or message of the film.

Connector

The Connector could research the film's director, writer, or actors, and share information about their backgrounds, influences, and other works. They could also connect the film to other works of literature or film that address similar themes or issues.

Investigator

The Investigator could research the historical or cultural context in which the film was made, and share information about relevant events, social movements, or political issues. They could also discuss how the film reflects or comments on these events or issues.

Artist

The Artist could analyze the film's visual and auditory elements, such as cinematography, sound design, or music. They could discuss how these elements contribute to the overall atmosphere or meaning of the film.

Researcher

The Researcher could research critical reviews or analyses of the film and share these with the group. They could also investigate the film's reception by audiences and critics and discuss how this reception has evolved over time.

Historian

The Historian could research the history of film as a medium and discuss how the film fits into this history. They could also investigate how the film's style, techniques, or themes have influenced other films or genres.

Assessing Student Learning in Literature Circles

THROUGHOUT THE LITERATURE circle experience, I found myself eagerly anticipating the final project. As someone who loves to express my creativity and who also loves literature, I was thrilled to have the opportunity to combine these passions. I knew that I wanted to create something that truly reflected my understanding of the text and showcased my unique perspective.

As I brainstormed ideas for the final project, I felt both excited and overwhelmed. There were so many possibilities, and I wanted to ensure that I chose something that would challenge me and allow me to demonstrate my learning in a meaningful way. With the help of my literature circle group and our teacher, I ultimately decided to create a visual representation of one of the key themes in the book.

As I worked on my project, I found that I was able to dive deeper into the text than I ever had before. I was able to explore the intricacies of the characters and their relationships, as well as the broader societal issues that the text addressed. The project allowed me to think critically about the book and consider its implications in a new way.

When it was finally time to present our projects, I was nervous but also incredibly proud. As I spoke about my piece, I felt a sense of accomplishment and validation. It was clear that my hard work had paid off, and I was thrilled to see that my literature circle group and teacher were impressed by what I had created.

Assessing student learning in literature circles can be challenging, but it is essential for understanding students' progress and growth. There are several methods for assessment, including both formative and summative assessments. Here are a few of the most common:

Self-Assessment

One way to assess student learning in literature circles is through self-assessment. After the completion of each circle, students can complete a self-assessment form that includes questions about their participation, contributions to the group, and comprehension of the text. This allows students to reflect on their learning and identify areas where they may need more support.

Strengths: Self-assessment helps students to take ownership of their learning and can encourage self-reflection. It is also a way for teachers to gather insight into students' understanding of the text.

Group Assessment

Another way to assess student learning in literature circles is through group assessment. Students in the group can evaluate each other's contributions to the discussion, including their preparedness, participation, and ability to listen and respond to others. This type of assessment encourages students to work collaboratively and fosters a sense of accountability.

Strengths: Group assessment encourages students to work collaboratively and can foster a sense of community within the classroom. It is also an opportunity for students to practice evaluating and giving feedback constructively.

One-on-One Conferences

Teachers can also use one-on-one conferences with students as a way to assess their learning in literature circles. During these conferences, teachers can ask questions about the text, the students' contributions to the discussion, and any areas where they may need additional support.

Strengths: One-on-one conferences allow teachers to gather insight into individual students' understanding of the text and provide targeted feedback.

Written Responses

Teachers can also ask students to write responses to literature circle discussions or prompts related to the text. These written responses can include summaries of the discussion, reflections on their own learning, or analysis of specific themes or characters.

Strengths: Written responses provide a way for teachers to assess students' understanding of the text in a more formalized way. It also allows students to practice written communication skills.

Performance Tasks

Performance tasks are another way to assess student learning in literature circles. These tasks may include creating a visual representation of a scene or character from the text, creating a short skit or play based on a scene or character, or writing a script for a short film or video.

Strengths: Performance tasks allow students to demonstrate their understanding of the text in a creative and engaging way. It also provides an opportunity for students to practice presentation skills and teamwork.

Literature Circle Project Ideas

THERE ARE PROBABLY as many project ideas as there are students. Don't let this list stifle your imagination – use it as a springboard for offering your students creativity and choice with how they represent their learning.

Character Analysis

Students could create a character analysis for a character from one of the books they read in the literature circle. This could include a written analysis of the character's traits, motivations, and relationships with other characters, as well as visual representations such as a character web or a character portrait.

Theme Exploration

Students could create a multimedia presentation that explores a theme that emerged from the books they read in the literature circle. This could include excerpts from the books, visual images, and written analysis that demonstrates how the theme is developed across the different texts.

Creative Writing

Students could write a creative piece inspired by one of the books they read in the literature circle. This could take the form of a short story, a poem, or a scene that expands upon a particular event or character from the book.

Literary Comparison

Students could create a Venn diagram or graphic organizer that compares and contrasts two or more of the books they read in the literature circle. This could include analysis of elements such as plot, character, setting, and theme.

Reader's Theater

Students could create a reader's theater script based on a scene from one of the books they read in the literature circle. They could perform the script for the class or record it as a video.

Book Review

Students could write a book review for one of the books they read in the literature circle. This could include an analysis of elements such as plot, character, setting, and theme, as well as a recommendation for other readers.

Podcast

Students could create a podcast episode that discusses one of the books they read in the literature circle. This could include interviews with classmates, analysis of literary elements, and personal reflections on the book.

Book Trailer

Students can create a book trailer for one of the books they read, using video, images, and music to convey the mood, tone, and themes of the book. They can use their understanding of the book's characters, setting, and plot to create an engaging and accurate representation of the book.

Literary Analysis

Students can write a literary analysis of one of the books they read, focusing on an aspect such as symbolism, metaphor, or imagery. They can use evidence from the text to support their analysis and use their understanding of literary devices and techniques to create a nuanced and insightful analysis.

Historical Research

Students can research the historical context of one of the books they read and create a presentation or report that contextualizes the book within its historical period. They can use their understanding of the book's themes and characters to make connections between the book and the historical events and movements of its time.

Book Club Discussion

Students can create a book club discussion guide for one of the books they read, using their understanding of the book's themes, characters, and plot to create thoughtful and engaging discussion questions. They can also provide prompts for creative activities, such as drawing or writing exercises, that relate to the book.

Providing Feedback to Students

PROVIDING FEEDBACK to students in a literature circle is a crucial aspect of the process. Feedback is an effective tool that helps students recognize their strengths and areas of improvement, allows them to learn from their mistakes, and helps them become better learners. Here are some ways teachers can provide feedback to students in a literature circle:

Written Feedback

Written feedback can be given in the form of comments on their literature circle journals, group discussion notes, or individual reading responses. This feedback can be provided after each literature circle meeting or at the end of the unit. Written feedback can be detailed, specific, and personalized, allowing students to reflect on their learning and progress.

Verbal Feedback

Verbal feedback can be given during literature circle meetings or in one-on-one conferences with students. During literature circle meetings, teachers can provide immediate feedback to students on their contributions to the group discussion, their understanding of the text, and their role in the literature circle. In one-on-one conferences, teachers can discuss student progress, address areas of concern, and provide suggestions for improvement.

Peer Feedback

Peer feedback allows students to give feedback to their peers and practice their critical thinking and communication skills. Teachers can assign students to provide feedback to their peers based on specific criteria, such as participation in the discussion, their contribution to group dynamics, and their understanding of the text.

Rubrics

Rubrics can be used to assess and provide feedback to students on their performance in the literature circle. Rubrics should be aligned with the learning objectives and should cover areas such as participation, discussion skills, and comprehension of the text. Rubrics provide a clear understanding of expectations, and students can use them as a tool for self-assessment.

Using Data to Inform Instruction

USING STUDENT DATA to inform instruction is a critical component of effective teaching, including in literature circles. By analyzing data collected during literature circles, teachers can identify areas where students need more support and instruction, as well as areas where they can be challenged. Here are some examples of how to use student data to inform instruction in literature circles:

Analyze Discussion Notes

During literature circles, teachers can collect notes on student discussions and use them to identify areas where students struggled or excelled. For example, if multiple students are struggling with making connections between the text and their own lives, the teacher may need to provide additional support in this area. Alternatively, if students are consistently engaging in thoughtful, insightful discussions, the teacher may need to provide more challenging texts or discussion prompts.

Review Written Responses

In addition to discussion notes, teachers can also collect and review written responses from students, such as journal entries or reading logs. These responses can provide insight into students' understanding of the text and their ability to analyze and interpret it. If a significant number of students are struggling with a particular concept or skill, such as making inferences or identifying theme, the teacher can provide additional instruction and practice in these areas.

Use Formative Assessments

Formative assessments, such as quizzes or exit tickets, can be used to gather data on students' understanding of specific concepts or skills. For example, if students are struggling with identifying the main idea of a text, the teacher can administer a short quiz or exit ticket to assess their understanding. Based on the results, the teacher can provide additional instruction or practice.

Track Reading Progress

By tracking students' reading progress throughout the literature circle, teachers can identify students who may need additional support or challenge. For example, if a student is consistently struggling to complete the assigned reading, the teacher may need to provide more scaffolding or support. On the other hand, if a student is consistently finishing the reading early and engaging in thoughtful discussions, the teacher may need to provide more challenging texts or discussion prompts.

Once the data has been collected and analyzed, teachers can use it to make informed instructional decisions. For example, if multiple students are struggling with a particular concept or skill, the teacher may need to provide additional instruction and practice in that area. Alternatively, if students are consistently engaging in thoughtful discussions, the teacher may need to provide more challenging texts or discussion prompts to push their thinking even further.

Troubleshooting Literature Circles

AS I SAT IN MY LITERATURE circle, I couldn't help but feel frustrated. Our group was struggling to communicate and work together. Everyone seemed to be talking over each other, and no one was really listening to what others had to say. It was overwhelming and confusing, and I wasn't even sure if I understood the book we were reading anymore.

At that moment, I felt like giving up. I thought that maybe literature circles just weren't for me. I was ready to walk away and ask my teacher if I could switch to a different group or do something else instead.

But before I could even ask, my teacher stepped in and offered some guidance. She reminded us of the expectations and goals of literature circles, and how important it was for each person to listen and contribute to the discussion. She helped us come up with strategies for taking turns and sharing our ideas in a respectful way.

Slowly but surely, our group started to turn things around. We listened to each other more and started asking questions to clarify misunderstandings. We even found common ground in some of our ideas about the book.

By the end of the literature circle, I felt proud of what we had accomplished. It wasn't easy, but with the help of our teacher, we were able to overcome our struggles and work together to deepen our understanding. I realized that literature circles are more than just a way to read a book - they are also an opportunity to learn (sometimes the hard way) how to communicate and collaborate effectively with others.

Literature circles can be an effective way to engage students in reading and discussion, but they can also present several challenges. Two common challenges that teachers may encounter are student resistance to participating in literature circles and group dynamics issues.

Student Resistance

Student resistance may be due to a variety of factors, such as feeling uncomfortable with public speaking or being shy around peers. It is important for teachers to address this issue early on by providing clear expectations for participation and emphasizing the importance of each student's contributions to the group. Teachers can also work with individual students to develop strategies to overcome their resistance, such as providing extra support or encouraging them to start with a smaller role in the group.

Group Dynamics

Group dynamics issues can arise when students have difficulty working together or when certain students dominate the conversation. To address this, teachers can implement strategies such as assigning clear roles and responsibilities for each group member, establishing clear guidelines for discussion, and monitoring group interactions. Teachers can also encourage students to use strategies such as active listening and respectful communication to ensure that everyone has a chance to participate.

Both of these challenges are covered in more detail in the next sections. It's worth noting that teachers may encounter other challenges as well, such as difficulty finding appropriate texts for the literature circles, scheduling conflicts, or difficulty balancing the needs of students with differing abilities within a group.

To overcome these challenges, teachers need to be flexible and creative in their approach, such as offering alternative texts or providing extra support for struggling readers. Effective planning and communication with students can also help to address these challenges and ensure that literature circles are successful for all students involved.

Student Resistance

STUDENT RESISTANCE to literature circles is a common challenge that teachers face. Some students may feel uncomfortable sharing their thoughts with others, while others may simply dislike reading. Fortunately, there are several strategies that teachers can use to help students overcome resistance and engage in the literature circle process:

Providing Choice

Students are more likely to engage with literature circles when they have a say in what they are reading. Providing students with a range of choices can help them find a book that they are interested in and invested in. When students are invested in the text, they are more likely to participate in the discussion.

Building Background Knowledge

Students who struggle with reading may feel resistant to literature circles because they lack the background knowledge necessary to understand the text. Teachers can help overcome this by providing students with background information about the text, such as historical context or key themes, and audio or video summaries before beginning the literature circle.

Modeling

Teachers can model effective discussion techniques and help students understand how to have a productive conversation. When students see their teacher participating in the discussion and using effective strategies, they are more likely to follow suit.

Gradual Release of Responsibility

Starting with small-group discussions or providing scaffolding for discussions can help students feel more comfortable participating in the literature circle process. Teachers can gradually release responsibility to the students as they become more comfortable with the process.

Providing Support

Some students may need extra support to feel comfortable in literature circles. Teachers can provide support through individual conferences, peer tutoring, or other interventions that meet students' individual needs.

Connecting to Students' Interests

Teachers can help students connect to the text by finding ways to relate it to students' interests and experiences. When students see the relevance of the text to their own lives, they are more likely to engage with the literature circle process.

Overcoming student resistance to literature circles requires a combination of strategies that build students' investment in the text, provide background knowledge, model effective discussion techniques, provide scaffolding and support, and connect to students' interests and experiences.

Group Dynamics Challenges

GROUP DYNAMICS CAN pose a challenge in literature circles, as different personalities, communication styles, and learning preferences can lead to conflicts or lack of engagement. Here are several strategies teachers can use to overcome these challenges:

Create a Positive Classroom Culture

A positive and respectful classroom culture can encourage students to feel safe and comfortable sharing their thoughts and ideas during literature circle discussions. Teachers can establish norms and expectations for behavior during discussions and model active listening and respectful communication.

Assign Roles

Assigning roles to each member of the literature circle can help balance participation and ensure that all students are engaged in the discussion. Roles could include discussion director, summarizer, vocabulary enricher, or connector, among others.

Rotate Roles

To further encourage engagement and ensure that all students are participating, teachers can rotate roles for each literature circle meeting. This allows students to develop different skills and perspectives, while also ensuring that everyone is accountable for their contribution to the discussion.

Use Icebreakers

At the beginning of each literature circle meeting, teachers can use icebreakers or warm-up activities to help students feel more comfortable with one another and build a sense of community. This could include simple activities such as sharing a favorite quote or discussing a recent news article.

Encourage Active Listening

Active listening is a critical skill for effective communication in literature circles. Teachers can encourage active listening by providing prompts or questions that require students to listen carefully to their peers' responses and ideas, such as asking follow-up questions or challenging assumptions.

Use Peer Feedback

Peer feedback can be a powerful tool for building positive group dynamics. Teachers can provide guidelines for constructive feedback and encourage students to give feedback on their peers' contributions to the literature circle discussion.

Provide Support For Struggling Students

For students who may struggle with group dynamics or participation, teachers can provide additional support such as individual check-ins or coaching on discussion skills. Teachers can also provide additional scaffolding for reading or discussion preparation for students who may need it.

What to Do When Literature Circles Aren't Working

EVEN WHEN TEACHERS have planned carefully and put a lot of effort into running literature circles, there may be times when the strategy just isn't working. Here are some actions teachers can take when they find themselves in this situation:

Reassess the Groupings

Sometimes the issue may be with the groupings. Consider rearranging the groups, or allowing students to choose their own groups to see if this helps with engagement and productivity.

Reassess the Text Choice

The text may not be resonating with students, or it may be too challenging. Consider choosing a different text that is more appropriate for the students' reading levels or interests.

Provide Additional Scaffolding

Students may need additional support to fully engage with the text. Provide extra materials, graphic organizers, or other scaffolds to help students understand the text and prepare for discussions.

Provide Additional Modeling

Students may need more modeling of how to effectively participate in literature circle discussions. Provide additional modeling or even mini-lessons on discussion skills to help students feel more comfortable and confident in their participation.

Provide More Guidance Roles

The roles assigned to students may not be clearly understood or may not be working effectively. Provide more guidance for each role, or even allow students to create their own roles based on what they feel is most important to the text.

Provide More Time

Sometimes students need more time to fully engage with the text and with their peers in discussions. Consider extending the length of the literature circle or even allowing more time within each session for discussions to take place.

Switch Up the Format

Traditional literature circles may not be working for all students. Consider trying a different format, such as a whole-class discussion or a small-group book club, to see if this helps with engagement and productivity.

It's important for teachers to remember that literature circles are not a one-size-fits-all strategy, and it's okay to make adjustments or even abandon the strategy altogether if it's not working for a particular group of students. Teachers should be open to feedback from their students and willing to make changes to ensure that all students are able to engage with the text and participate effectively in discussions.

Conclusion

I HAVE TO SAY, I REALLY enjoyed participating in the literature circle. At first, I wasn't quite sure what to expect and was a bit scared to share my thoughts and opinions with others. But as we started reading and discussing the book, I found myself getting more and more excited about our group meetings.

It was so interesting to hear everyone's different perspectives on the characters and plot. I loved how we all brought our own unique experiences and ideas to each meeting. Even when we disagreed, it was always in a respectful and thoughtful way.

I also appreciated how our teacher gave us the freedom to choose our own roles within the group. It was awesome to be able to take on a leadership role and guide our discussions. And I loved how we were able to be creative with our final project and show our learning in a unique and meaningful way.

Overall, I feel like the literature circle was an incredibly valuable experience for me. I not only improved my reading and thinking skills, but I also developed stronger relationships with my classmates and gained a deeper appreciation for literature. I can't wait to do more literature circles in the future!

Throughout this book, we explored the many benefits and strengths of literature circles. We discussed how they can promote critical thinking and engagement, while also providing opportunities for collaboration and differentiation.

We looked at various strategies for preparing and running successful literature circles, including text selection, group formation, and role assignment. We also examined ways to scaffold reading and discussion skills, as well as methods for assessing student learning and providing feedback.

We discussed the challenges that can arise during literature circles, such as student resistance and group dynamics issues, and offered solutions for overcoming them. We also explored the importance of using student data to inform instruction and making adjustments when literature circles are not working.

By implementing the strategies and techniques outlined in this book, teachers can create a dynamic and engaging learning environment where students can develop critical thinking and communication skills while exploring literature in a meaningful way.

Future Directions

IN RECENT YEARS, LITERATURE circles have gained popularity as an effective approach to teaching and learning literature in the classroom. However, as with any educational practice, there is always room for growth and evolution. Here are a few possible future directions for literature circles:

Incorporating Technology

As technology becomes more prevalent in the classroom, there is an opportunity to leverage it to enhance literature circles. This could include using online discussion boards or video conferencing to facilitate remote literature circles, or incorporating digital tools such as annotation software to support close reading.

Diversifying Text Options

While traditional literature circles often center around novels, there is potential to broaden the types of texts used in literature circles. This could include incorporating graphic novels, poetry, or non-fiction works to engage students with different interests and learning styles.

Incorporating Social Justice Themes

Literature circles can be a powerful tool for exploring social justice issues and encouraging critical thinking. In the future, teachers may choose to intentionally incorporate texts with social justice themes, or provide students with opportunities to select and discuss texts that are meaningful to them in this regard.

Focusing on Global Literature

As the world becomes increasingly interconnected, there is value in exposing students to literature from around the globe. In the future, literature circles may incorporate more works from international authors or texts that explore global issues.

Overall, the future of literature circles is exciting and full of potential. By continuing to evolve and adapt this approach to teaching and learning literature, educators can ensure that it remains a valuable tool for years to come.

Final Thoughts on the Importance of Literature Circles

ONE OF THE KEY BENEFITS of literature circles is that they allow students to take ownership of their learning. By working in small groups, students have the opportunity to choose the books they want to read and to engage in meaningful discussions with their peers. This approach also allows for differentiated instruction as students can choose books that match their interests and reading abilities.

Another advantage of literature circles is that they foster a love of reading. When students have a say in the books they read and are able to engage in discussions with their peers, they are more likely to be motivated to read. Literature circles also allow students to explore different genres and authors, which can help them develop a deeper appreciation for literature.

In addition to promoting a love of reading, literature circles help to build important skills that are essential for success in the 21st century. Students learn to think critically about the literature they read and to communicate their ideas effectively with others. They also learn to collaborate with their peers, which is an important skill for success in both academic and professional settings.

Finally, literature circles help to create a community of readers in the classroom. When students come together to discuss literature, they are able to share their thoughts and ideas with their peers. This creates a sense of belonging and encourages students to support each other in their reading and learning.

As teachers, it is important to continue to explore and implement literature circles in our classrooms, so that we can provide our students with the best possible learning experiences.

Further Reading

BROWNLIE, FAYE. *Grand Conversations, Thoughtful Responses: A Unique Approach to Literature Circles*. Portage & Main Press, 2019.

Daniels, Harvey. *Literature Circles: Voice and Choice in Book Clubs and Reading Groups*. Stenhouse Publishers, 2002.

Moeller, Marc, and Moeller, Victor. *Literature Circles That Engage Middle and High School Students*. Taylor & Francis, 2016.

Moeller, Marc, and Moeller, Victor. *Socratic Seminars and Literature Circles*. Taylor & Francis, 2013.

Morris, Brooke, and Perlenfein, Deborah. *Literature Circles: The Way to Go and How to Get There*. Teacher Created Resources, Incorporated, 2002.

Rogers, Warren and Leochko, Dave. *Literature Circles: Tools and Techniques to Inspire Reading Groups*. Portage & Main Press, 2002.

Don't miss out!

Visit the website below and you can sign up to receive emails whenever Cheryl Angst publishes a new book. There's no charge and no obligation.

https://books2read.com/r/B-A-SBAY-IVCJC

BOOKS 2 READ

Connecting independent readers to independent writers.

About the Author

Cheryl Angst has been teaching in the classroom for over twenty-five years. With a Masters in curriculum and instruction, her passion centers around finding tips, tricks, and strategies to enhance her practice.

Cheryl is a firm believer that learning should be fun for both the students and the teacher. If it isn't engaging, or doesn't spark joy, it's likely able to be done differently.

The "Quick Reads for Busy Educators" series is designed to maximize the precious time educators have. Each book is short enough to be read in an hour or less, but contains a wealth of information on the topic. Some books are overviews of strategies and approaches (enough to help educators decide if it's for them) and some are deeper dives into specific aspects of those larger approaches. This allows busy educators to grab the information they need quickly and efficiently.

If there's a topic you'd like to see covered in the "Quick Reads" series, please let us know!